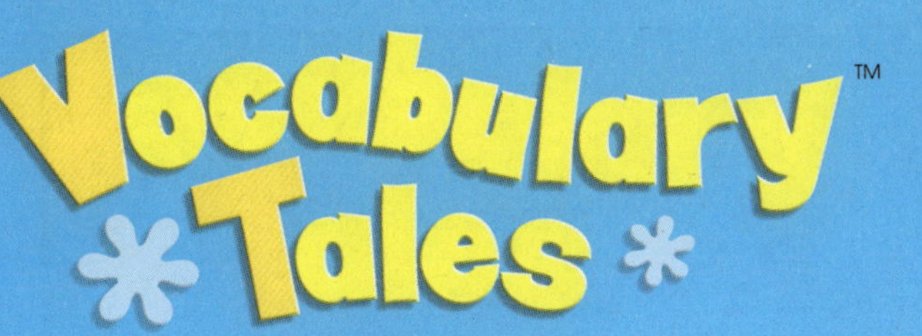

Katie the Caterpillar

by Pamela Chanko
illustrated by Laura Ferraro Close

SCHOLASTIC INC.
New York • Toronto • London • Auckland • Sydney
Mexico City • New Delhi • Hong Kong • Buenos Aires

Designed by Maria Lilja
ISBN-13: 978-0-545-08873-2 • ISBN-10: 0-545-08873-9

First printing, November 2008

12 11 10 9 8 7 6 5 4 3 2 1 8 9 10 11 12 13/0

Building Vocabulary With This Book

This book contains eight key words that are important for all children to know. Read the story straight through for enjoyment. Then read it again, pausing to define and discuss each key word. Follow-up the tale with the fun activities on pages 14–16. When you're done, celebrate—kids will have added eight great words to their vocabularies!

Katie the caterpillar was tired of being little. She couldn't wait to be big. *But what will I do when I grow up?* thought Katie. She decided to ask the other insects what they were going to do.

"What will you do when you grow up?" Katie asked Little Cicada.

"I will **chirp** all night," he said.

"Oh," said Katie. "I could never do that."

KEY WORD: **hive**

Simple Definition: a home for bees

Sample Sentence: I sometimes see bees buzzing around the *hive* in my backyard.

"What will you do when you grow up?" Katie asked Little Bumblebee.

"I will make honey in a **hive**," he said.

"Oh," said Katie. "I could never do that."

“What will you do when you grow up?” Katie asked Little Grasshopper.

“I will leap from leaf to leaf,” he said.

“Oh,” said Katie. “I could never do that.”

KEY WORD: **camouflage**

Simple Definition: a coloring or covering that makes an animal look like its surroundings

Sample Sentence: Polar bears use *camouflage* to blend in with snowbanks.

"What will you do when you grow up?" Katie asked Little Walkingstick.

"I will use **camouflage** to look like a twig," he said.

"Oh," said Katie. "I could never do that."

"What will you do when you grow up?" Katie asked Little Beetle.

"I will shine like a jewel," he said.

"Oh," said Katie. "I could never do that."

KEY WORD: **cart**

Simple Definition: to carry

Sample Sentence: Poor David had to *cart* the giant pumpkin all the way home from the patch.

"What will you do when you grow up?" Katie asked Little Ant.

"I will **cart** huge pieces of food to my anthill," he said.

"Oh," said Katie. "I could never do that."

KEY WORD: creep

Simple Definition: to move slowly and quietly

Sample Sentence: I like to *creep* up on my little brother and say, "Boo!"

"What will you do when you grow up?" Katie asked Little Centipede.

"I will use my legs to **creep** all around," he said.

"Oh," said Katie. "I could never do that."

KEY WORD: **glow**

Simple Definition: to give off a low light

Sample Sentence: Candles *glow* when they are lit.

"What will you do when you grow up?" Katie asked Little Firefly.

"I will **glow** in the dark," he said.

"Oh," said Katie. "I could never do that."

Katie was sad. "I'll never be special like other bugs," she said. She just wanted to be alone. So she built a little home. Then she crawled inside it.

KEY WORD: emerge

Simple Definition: to come out into the open

Sample Sentence: The sleeping bear will *emerge* from its cave in early spring.

The other insects were worried about Katie. "She's been in there so long!" they said. "Do you think she will ever **emerge**?"

At last, the insects heard a flutter of wings. It was Katie! She was all grown up and she looked beautiful! "Wow! What a **metamorphosis**! You are a butterfly!" the insects said. "We could never do that!"

Meaning Match

insect words

Listen to the definition. Then go to the WORD CHEST and find a vocabulary word that matches it.

1. the high sound that an insect or a bird makes
2. a home for bees
3. a coloring or covering that makes an animal look like its surroundings
4. to carry
5. to move slowly and quietly
6. to give off a low light
7. to come out into the open
8. a big change

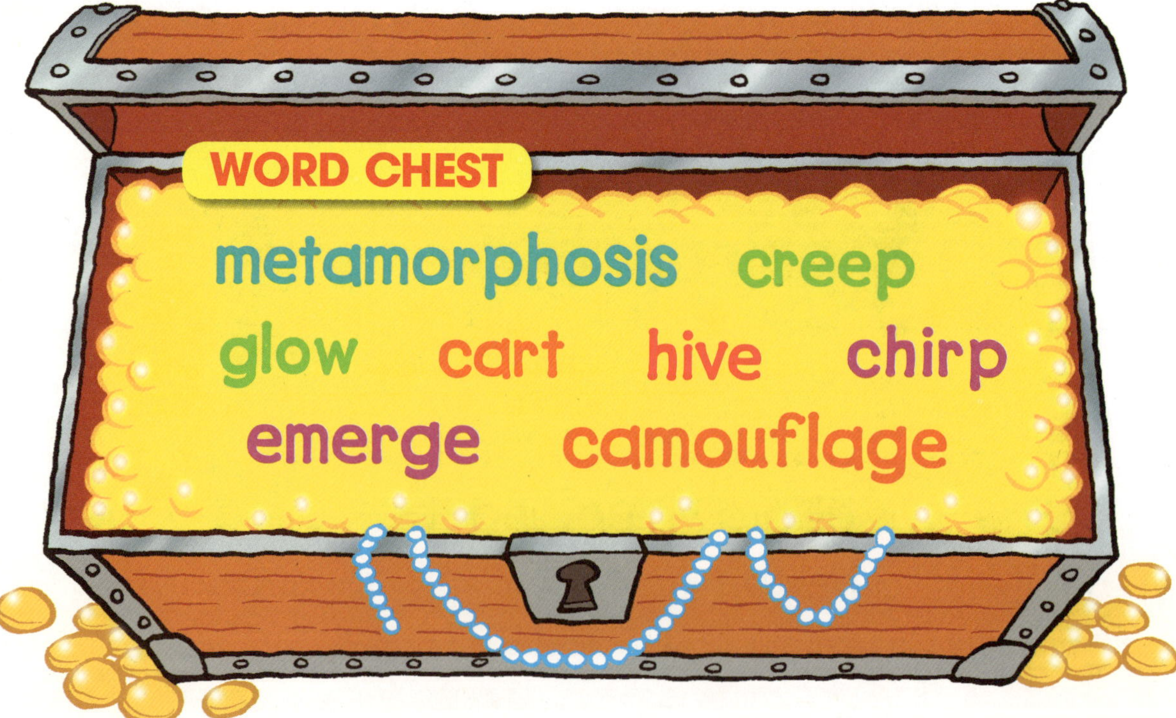

Answers: 1. chirp 2. hive 3. camouflage 4. cart 5. creep 6. glow 7. emerge 8. metamorphosis

Vocabulary Fill-ins

insect words

Listen to the sentence. Then go to the WORD BOX and find the best word to fill in the blank.

WORD BOX

creep	metamorphosis	hive	glow
emerge	camouflage	cart	chirp

1. My tadpole turned into a frog. What a ________!

2. Crickets often ________ at night.

3. Green fish hide in seaweed. That is called ________.

4. Fireflies ________ in the night sky.

5. Gina had to ________ a big box of books all the way to school.

6. I saw an ant ________ across the kitchen table.

7. Susan was so sick that she did not ________ from her room for the whole day!

8. The bees flew in and out of their ________.

Answers: 1. metamorphosis 2. chirp 3. camouflage 4. glow 5. cart 6. creep 7. emerge 8. hive

Vocabulary Questions

insect words

Listen to each question. Think about it. Then answer.

1. Pretend you are a butterfly about to **emerge** from your cocoon. What will you do when you get outside?
2. Can you imitate a bird's **chirp**? What does it sound like?
3. If a bug wanted to use **camouflage** to hide on your shirt, what color would it need to be?
4. Can you think of an animal that goes through a **metamorphosis**? Tell about how it changes.
5. What kinds of creatures can **creep**? Make a list.
6. What are some things that **glow** in the sky at night?
7. Have you ever had to **cart** something a long way? Tell about it.
8. Bees live in **hives**. Can you think of some other animal homes?

Extra: Can you think of some more insect words? Make a list.